MW01487565

To Rosie Ma

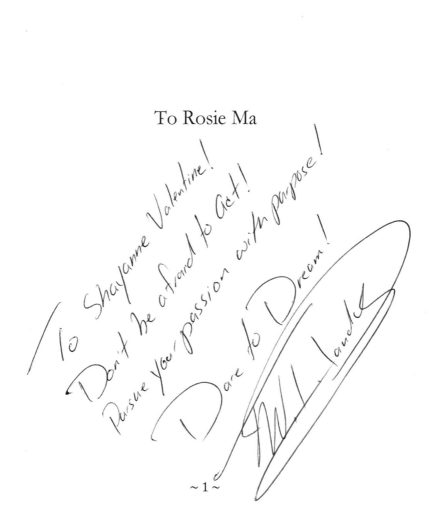

To Shayanne Valentine!
Don't be afraid to Act!
Pursue your passion with purpose!

Dare to Dream!

Forward by:
Dr. William E. Flippin
Senior Pastor, Greater Piney Grove Baptist Church
Atlanta, Georgia

Grammar always gave me trouble to master in my early childhood education. When the teacher would ask the class to conjugate verbs, I would shutter. Great tragedy would grip my heart when my written work was returned to me with red marker written across the page. I had not mastered syntax. I had not learned to appreciate subjects, verbs, adjectives, adverbs and grammar.

Life has a way of teaching the grammar lessons we dreaded in our childhood. Minister Wendel Dandridge has presented us with wisdom far beyond his chronological years. He helps us to understand that where God has placed a comma in our lives, we dare not place a period. It is normal to assume that the author has a long life in front of him. Thus, how can he know so much about life and living?

Since coming to Atlanta as a freshman at Morehouse College Wendel has served our church. It almost amuses me each time we gather for worship when I sense Minister Dandridge absorbing my style and model for ministry. He has told me that "Excellence is his standard". His growth and maturity is evident in his solid and sincere energy in ministry. He believes strongly in hard work and sacrifice. He combines determination along with attaining a quality education. These traits place Minister Dandridge on the playing field that provides a bright future. *After the Comma: A Grammar Lesson on Life* offers a fresh look at the journey we call life from the eyes of a young scholar of religion and psychology.

You will be engaged in the interesting and dramatic symbolism that Wendel Dandridge uses to make his points come alive and relevant for your life today!

Forward by:
Dr. Philip Dunston
Professor of Religious Studies
Clark Atlanta University

After the Comma: A Grammar Lesson on Life, is a fascinating answer to an age old question, how can I live an effective, prosperous and blessed life? Wendel Dandridge has a clever and witty mind. He uses grammatical syntax from the English language to provide practical tools for victorious living.

I am amazed at the degree of knowledge, skill and life experiences Wendel has obtained in a short life span. What is more amazing is his ability to articulate this message in such a way that anyone can follow these life strategies to acquire victory in every area of life. He understands how difficult it is to be successful in life without the necessary guidance. It is enriching to me to see one of my best students engage in providing quality life coaching for any player who wants to win.

The life coaching tips and strategies in the book are time tested and Holy Spirit approved. Understanding the three F's, Focus, Faith and Favor, will give any life player, at any skill level, the ability to become a professional at winning the game of life.

The title of the book and throughout its pages, Wendel Dandridge exhorts you to appreciate the punctuation marks of life. Life does not end after the comma. For those who have had comma experiences, there is life after the comma. The story is not over until God says it's over. He motivates you to continue living and reading until the period. Moreover, for the life player that believes in the providential destiny and purposes of God, even the period does not signal the end.

Forward by:
Pastor Michael W. Palmer
New Friendship Baptist Church
Baltimore, Maryland

In my twenty years of experience in law enforcement, corrections, and crime prevention, I have had my share of conflict and conversations with young men who seemed intent on destroying their lives by engaging in illegal, immoral, and immature activities and behaviors. I came to learn that many of these young men were good people who, unfortunately, lacked a positive male influence. They were in desperate need of both discipline and direction. Unable to resist the urge to address this need, I found myself fulfilling the role of mentor to some of these men.

As I later transitioned from policing to pastoring, I realized God had anointed me with the gift of mentoring to positively influence the lives of men in the church and community; especially young pastors and ministers. God has afforded me the opportunity to mentor and befriend young men in ministry who possess an intense desire to attain excellence in kingdom building. These young men are not only encouraging to their peers and subordinates, but are also inspiring to the "seasoned saints" in the church. W.T. Dandridge is one of these very impressive young men.

W. T. Dandridge is sincere, self-sacrificing, and sensitive to the needs of the body of Christ. He works tirelessly to create a variety of avenues to minister to those who are saved and those who are in need of salvation. His continued courage to be transparent about his personal journey (a trait he inherited from his wonderful mother) has been a key to his success and will, without a doubt, enhance his ministry and future growth, both personally and professionally. Each of these distinctive qualities will become apparent as you read *After the Comma: A Grammar Lesson on Life*.

In this book, W.T. Dandridge uses a unique and creative approach to present us with inspiring information and practical advice that can assist the believer in living a life that is increasingly progressive and productive. Furthermore, he challenges us to expect more from God and to excel beyond the obstacles and manmade limitations we are certain to encounter. Prepare yourself! *After the Comma: A Grammar Lesson on Life* places you on the path to transformation. Enjoy the journey!

Table of Contents

THE COMMA

After the Comma: Your Story Isn't Over

Intro: I preached a sermon in 2007 that touched the lives of many individuals. I am at a point in my life where I am focused on preaching and ministering messages that will do people good. I am focused on ministering messages that will motivate persons to obtain the reward that has already been predestined for them. This sermon in particular was a message that I knew was going to be abnormal for me. At one point in my preaching style I was a stereotypical Baptist preacher. Throughout my ministry I was taught I had to be in the pulpit standing behind the "sacred desk". I was challenged on this particular occasion to do something different… literally teach the congregation.

To this day, those who were in attendance still make reference to that sermon and always make mention of the fact that their lives were changed. I believe with all my heart that there needs to be a shift in the way we do ministry. We have been called not to talk at the people or to the people, but with the people. Since that day I have developed a very intimate style of delivery where I attempt to make every person in the audience feel as though I am talking to them. I believe transparency and ministry go hand and hand. It is my goal in this second writing of mine to truly be transparent with you, the reader, in an effort to introduce a new way to approach thinking and life. I do not want you to feel as though you are reading a book, but rather feel that I am in the room with you, right now, coaching you through this thing we call life.

When I do spiritual life coaching and counseling sessions I sit with all my clients. I do not sit away from them as if I am observing them, but rather I position myself just as a true friend or confidant would. What I did with this sermon in particular was took the very basic principle of grammar and punctuation and painted an imagery associated with reality. Sometimes we can make life principles too difficult and too complicated to understand. With all of our big words, degrees and pedigrees, so often do we miss the opportunity to touch the common person. I have to catch myself at times because I am considered educated. I have letters in front and behind my name. I have a very extensive library. I sometimes forget about humbling myself and my ministry to reach the common person.

If you take note, some of Jesus' most powerful lessons were taught by way of parables and stories. He did not have an intro, three points, a close and a Hammond organ, but He gave us great lessons with examples and occurrences from everyday life. When I preached the sermon "After the Comma" in 2007 it was my goal to reach people in the same manner Jesus did. It was my desire to touch every heart and person in the room from the youngest to the eldest. That sermon changed my preaching style and my perspective on ministry. As a result I was lead to expound on this sermon in book form, thus leading to this finished project. It is my prayer that these words would inspire you to take the basic principles outlined and make them practicable in your everyday lives.

It is one thing to listen to the words and instructions of the universe; however it is another thing to actually work with the instructions given. Imagine a father who is experiencing for the first time putting together an expensive baby crib. With millions of pieces, parts, screws, nuts, boards and his wife standing over his shoulder; the frustration he experiences of knowing where to start. My admonishment to him, as well as to you who have chosen to embark on the journey of life, is that you would start with the blueprint and instructions. From here you can go piece by piece until you accomplish your goal. This book is not written for those who want a "no assembly required" life, but rather for those who are willing to heed to the instructions that will help you walk in your destiny. Understand that God did promise you a rainbow, but God also promised you the flood. The premise behind this book is that God places us in the classroom we call life to learn multiple lessons.

We must first enter into the mindset that we are constantly experiencing life and reality. It is from life and reality that we should also be learning. One thing that I teach constantly is not to look at the situation on the surface, but rather try to uncover the lesson that is to be learned in the experience. So often we get caught up in situations. We do not take the time to just sit back and observe the lesson in the experience. It is in the process of learning and observing that God is able to show us and teach us how to handle the punctuations of life. In my sermon "After the Comma" it was the first time I had every done something outside of my preaching comfort zone. I literally set a stage for the message that Sunday morning. I went to the church the night before, moved the sacred desk, moved the communion table, set up a teacher's desk, and placed some student desks at the altar. The next morning I walked the congregation through the classroom. I had tables and chairs in front of the church. I had a teacher's desk, and as the sermon progressed I was able to make my way through the classroom illustrating the importance of understanding the will of God in our lives.

I anticipate and wish for you to walk with me again in this book. The words on the following pages are words from my heart that I hope and pray will minister to any and all aspects of your life that you seem to be facing. Thank you for taking the time to read. Thank yourself for the desire to want change in your life. Thank God for the opportunity to be enlightened. Enjoy!

CHAPTER 1

Understanding Your Story:

Dream Mentality Vs. Destiny Mentality

Dream Mentality will always have you in a fairy tale state.

There is nothing more detrimental than living a life of wishful thinking. I come in to contact with many people in my ministry, counseling and life coaching. Many of them are individuals who "wish" for things to happen in their lives. It reminds me of multiple Disney fairy tales where the main character wants and desires something so bad, to the point where they dream about it daily. There may be some white clouds that come out of your head daily and play for you a movie of your wishes. Many people get caught up in this type of thought. Many stay in this mindset until they wake up and realize that wishes do not happen without action.

One of my favorite Disney stories growing up was Aladdin. Although there were many things that Aladdin desired in his life, his wishes did not come to a full fruition until he left his current state of reality (the slums) and entered a world of adventure and possibility. In order to truly obtain the wishes and great things the universe has in store for you, action is necessary. Rest assured there is provision in the action. If we are willing to create the adventure, instead of imagining the fairy tale, the universe will give you the desires of your heart. How many people have you come in contact with who talk a good game about what they want, but never make it their reality? I encourage you to begin the adventure that will ultimately help you obtain your wishes. Get to a position in your life where you are not satisfied with the thought and tale about the genie, but go on the adventure to find your genie. When you find him do not settle for just three wishes. Tell the universe all the desires of your heart and then ask for guidance and direction as you go on your expedition to destiny.

You may find yourself caught up in the fairy tale of expectancy instead of acknowledging what reality truly is. If I can revisit the story of Aladdin there is one thing I could note that was always in the back of Aladdin's mind. Regardless of his relationship with the princess, the new clothes and fancy camels, or the fact that he had been placed on a pedestal of honor and power, reality was that he was still a peasant. Aladdin never lost the reality that there were still real issues that he had to deal with. In your own situations, you must learn how to be real with yourself about the things hindering you and holding you back from obtaining your wishes. Truth be told, you have issues. Some of those issues are uncontrollable and some of those issues are controlled.

My challenge to you is to identify what reality in your life is holding you back from moving forward. Whether it is an addiction, a relationship, a job, a childhood experience, a religious encounter, a social injustice or a financial road block, you must identify reality in your life and address it. Do not go through life giving off the appearance that you do not have any issues! I remember a young lady I dated back in high school. When I brought her home to meet my family she was asked the question from my mother, "What kind of issues do you have?" I assume in her attempt to impress, she said she did not have any issues. To this day my mother and I laugh about that statement because clearly she had some issues! The moment you are able to properly identify your problems and your dilemmas, the more quickly you will be able to address them, solve them and then move forward.

A dream is just a figment of your imagination until action is put to it. At the point of action it is then considered a vision. When I think of the "I Have a Dream" speech by Martin Luther King Jr. I recall a portion of the speech, which makes reference to him "not going to the mountain top with you". There is a reason the bible declares to us that your "Old men shall dream dreams and your young men shall see visions". There comes a position in your life where you ultimately determine, is God showing you a dream or showing you a vision?

This may be a hard pill to swallow, but everything that God shows you are not meant for you to experience. I want you to meditate on that for a minute. You can get so excited in thinking that everything God shows you is meant for you to obtain. There are countless stories throughout history that demonstrate God showing a dream but allowing someone else to reap the vision of that dream. It takes a strong spiritual person to go to God and ask "Is what you are showing me… you want me to have?" It is a very hard reality to understand that although God wants us to have and obtain great things in life, everything God shows you is not meant for you to obtain. Sometimes it is meant for you to have the dream, place things in motion, so someone else can build on it and make it apart of their vision. With vision you always see the end result and you will most likely hold the end result.

My encouragement is that you move beyond a lazy dream and move in to a vision with action. One phrase that will kill your vision is "Let me think about it". Or if I can put it in the context of this book, "Let me dream about it". Let me waddle in the feelings that I get by just thinking about it. When I am life coaching I always propose people to do something different with their lives. Some of the main responses I get are along the lines of this dream concept. I have met many people who are comfortable with just the dream. People who like what success looks like but do nothing to find out what success feels like! You know people who always talk about making it big and people who constantly say "wait until I…." Understand people who are comfortable with a dream will do exactly that… dream. One thing I have learned in working with the power of thought and the law of attraction is when you hold mental pictures in your head, your body can not tell the difference if you have actually received it or not. When we dream and think about that new job, new marriage, successful business and so forth, we fake ourselves out to believe and feel that we already have it. Don't you want to get to a position in your life where you can go from feeling to obtaining?

Do not sit on a lazy dream/vision. Do you honestly believe thinking and feeling good about anything is going to bring it in your life? You must learn how to position, or reposition, yourself to feel it and receive it. I was able to learn early in life and success the law of action. Have you ever had the realization, after receiving your heart's desires, "I could have done this a long time ago"? When you are honest with yourself you understand that you are what's holding YOU back. I placed the second you in capital letters because it is the little you holding the greater YOU back! I do not want you to enter into a place of regret or guilt, because that is not what this book is intended to accomplish. Rather I want you to be honest and discover if you would be a lot better off, if you just moved beyond self? Part of this book is designed to help you smoothly transition through life. You are not living, if you are not moving. You are not obtaining greatness or success if you are not choosing to move. You must move in order to position yourself to receive. One of the best words of advice I can give you is not to get caught up in feelings. Feelings and emotions will only give you a mirage or osmosis of your dreams. Reality says that in order for you to find that dream you will have to go on the adventure to discover it!

Thoughts about your dream only make you feel good… living out the dream helps you to experience good. The feel good dilemma is one that affects all of us. You must understand the power that feelings have over you. Many are not motivated by their passions, desires, or wills, but rather many of the things we do and experience are based on how we feel. I remember teaching a lecture on the power of perception. One thing I have come to realize about many persons is that they do not know what true reality is. Rather I propose that we live in and are influenced by our perceptions of reality. That perception is what our motivation becomes. How often can you say you genuinely did something because you were responding to the reality of the situation? In most cases you will respond based on your gathered perceptions about the situation.

As I stated in the previous chapter you should want to do more than just feel good about a situation. Make a note that there are emotions and feeling that hinder you from obtaining the things the universe has to offer you. There must be a desire to experience in your life. Before I began writing this book I was very cognizant not to allow certain feelings, i.e. frustration, stress, loneliness, disappointment, and sacredness, hinder me from truly experiencing the process of writing. Can you identify cases in your life where you were unable to live because there was a feeling hindering your liberation? Face the facts: you could not experience a loving relationship because you felt a since of insecurity. You could not experience running a good business because you felt inadequate and unconfident in your business knowledge. You did not experience the educational matriculation because you felt as though your life management skills would not be conducive to the curriculum. You did not experience the true manifestation of God in your life because you still feel as though you have a lot of personal work to do in order to make yourself worthy of God's favor.

I encourage you not to be misled and lied to by the misperceptions of your feelings! Your feelings should become the compass and thermometer for your experience… not the voice of direction.

I had a huge problem with my life. I was the type of person who would "Write the vision and make it plain". I would tell people about things I was going to do in my life, and how I had planned for it to happen. They would say, "Wow Wendel! This is going to be great!" In my mind and on paper it was great. If you read it, you would say to yourself there is no way possible this plan will not be successful. However, my greatest problem was those things always stayed on paper. In my bed room, my briefcase and my office I still have piles of papers with ideas, plans and outlines on them.

Following through is a habit you need to practice in life. So often do you get consumed in the planning, outlining, structuring and printing that you never actually get to manifest. I have experienced a few network marking positions and have always been successful with them. While in these businesses I have learned people who plan without action will never get success. Do not confuse my message, I want you to plan and be particular. I want you to write your visions out and focus on them daily. I want you to have structure and an outline to make things happen. I want you to formulate a blue print and a road map to follow. But what I do not want you to do is forget to act! If you know you have things in your closet you never acted on…. Close this book now and go get them. Pull out every list, outline, picture, book, sticky note, and brown bag you found yourself writing on at lunch. As you read, look at the creativity the universe has blessed you with and then ask yourself the question "Why have I not done this?" Understand everything in existence today came from the creative juices of someone's mind.

Destiny mentality will place you in an autobiographical state.

The question regarding your purpose in life is really a question if you are living someone else's story? Are you living through the life of someone else's experience, or are you writing your own autobiography? When you get into a destiny mentality you will understand your life and adventure is unique and particular to you. You have been placed on this earth, in this prescribed amount of time, and in the environment you cohabitate for a particular purpose.

I believe people have stopped writing biographies because there are not many people who live a life so different that anyone wants to document it. When you go to the library and see all the biographies that have been published, notice how these individuals stood out from the rest of society in some way, shape or form. We have lost our responsibility to originality. Most of us are guilty for trying to immolate the life of another individual. When will we learn to find our own destiny without comparing it or trying to make it like someone else's path? You must discover who you are through your own journey. The reason you do not know who we are is because you are looking in someone else's mirror.

When you look at yourself you can point out the majority of things you do, do not come from your original creative mind. There may be some of you reading this and saying, "I know who I am!", "I'm not trying to be like anyone else", "I know how to be creative!", "I am original!" For those who are saying this I challenge you to: go to your kitchen and see how many of someone else's recipes you are using; go to your closet and discover how many cloths and shoes you bought because they were advertised to you as making you look good; go to your job/office and ask yourself if you are really there because you are passionate about what you are doing or are you there because you want to be like the person in the corner office and this is where you have to get started; walk into your house, or look around your apartment and ask, is this décor me? Or did I try to create the look of the most recent magazine? Look at all the aspects of your life and ask the questions: "Is this really me and does this truly display my originality and creativity?" Some of you will say, Wendel there is only but so much you can create without repeating the thoughts and ideas of someone else. My response to you is that you are robbing the universe when you do not manifest what has been formulated in your creative consciousness.

There is nothing wrong with looking at the example and experiences of others, but at some point you need to create your own footprints in the sand of time. Learn to live a life where people will look at you and not wonder, but look at you and know that what you bring to the world is unique to everyone else. Let them look to you as a source of creativity, originality and inspiration. Not that they would inspire to be like you, but rather that they inspire to find what you have found: the power "to be" without hindrance or influence.

Destiny mentality will place you in the play!

As I stated in my previous chapters we get caught up in watching the adventure of someone else's that we never enter into our own story line. I remember growing up watching my twin sister sit in front of the television for hours a day watching movies! I am not talking about little flicks either. Sometimes she would watch Titanic two and three times a day! For many people they stay in fairy tale mode for the majority of their lives. We have all grown up thinking one day the unicorn would come take us to our prince charming or that we would somehow fly like spider man and get the girl in the end. However these childhood fantasies only matured into adult sized dreams. The stories we consistently watch are the same stories you will make comparison to in your life. In the long term you never receive anything you perceive.

With all the endeavors I have started and accomplished in life, I have found that there are two types of people who will always be around. There are those who have never done what you have done before; and will claim you cannot do it. Then there are those who will watch what you are doing, wanting to do what you do, but never once ask how you did it or even what they can do in order to get it done in their lives. At one point I was both of these individuals. I did not believe in the power of potential. I was at a position in my life where I was caught in the rat race. I thought the only way to be successful was to model my life after someone else who was already successful. It was not until I wanted to be set apart. It was not until I wanted to be remembered as a unique individual that my destiny quest began. Learn to harness the law of attachment and detachment. Know that what is in your environment is indicative to the type of person you are. Understand the concept of you being and becoming the company you keep. If you could take an inventory of the people you have in your life, could you say they are at the same place you are in your life? Once you answer this question ask yourself if they are helping you get to where you have to go or moving in the same direction you want to go? I want you to get out there and in the game. Get to a position in your life where you can say you are living and not just watching life go by.

Destiny mentality will always move you from wishing to working.

The goal of this book is to do more than just give you some good words of advice. As a spiritual life coach I would do a horrible job if I just gave my clients good words and never offered any sound or practical method of accomplishing their goals. Destiny thinkers always make a plan for their adventure and then follow it! I feel sorry for the individual who has a plan in their hands but refuses to follow it with their feet. Do not get caught in life just holding the map. There will be millions of people who will read the pages of this book and will never get out there and do a thing with the advice I am giving. I am willing to suggest after reading this chapter that you begin working towards your goals. At the beginning of this adventure I was going to make "After the Comma" just a book. Then I was lead to make this a workbook. I want you to feel and become engaged in this process of enlightenment. By the end of this book, after having completed the process, you will be propelled to experience a better life and reap a better lifestyle. In order for you to go after the comma, you must move beyond the before.

There are some things you are going to have to leave in the past. There are some people you will leave in the past as well. There are some old habits that will have to be left behind. The work will take a lot of your time and a lot of your energy but I ask you if your treasure is worth your adventure? If I can be transparent, there was a time in my destiny quest where I faced depression. It is actually something I still struggle with today, even in the process of writing this book. I have come to realize some of the greatest Destiny quests are lonely quests… but the treasure is worth it. I am not saying there will not be people or things that will accompany you on your journey; however there will be a great number of times where you will have to go alone. Or you may have to steal away from those in your environment in order to do an exercise that will help expand the consciousness of your adventure. Sometimes, after a weekend of lectures, singing, and conferences I have to do some "me" things. Some individual's company is not going to be conducive for your personal growth. You must understand the work involved getting to your future, and the sacrifices are what will help you get to that next level.

Destiny mentality will have you stop reading and admiring someone else's dreams and accomplishments and will help you obtain your own.

There is no greater feeling in life than saying "I did it". The power of ownership moves beyond obtaining a physical possession. Many people try to supplement their internal wants and wishes by trying to fulfill them with empirical possessions. As you read this book ask yourself the question; "What do I own?" But please do not answer the similar question of "What do I have?", but think in the sense of accomplishments and life. I meet and come in contact with people who never feel a sense of accomplishment in their lives. One cause behind this, in my opinion, is that people never own anything. There was a time where I felt as though I needed to have things in order to feel as though I was somebody. I would look at celebrities and other influential figures and equate who they were by what they had. The effect behind this was that I started to equate who I was by what I had. I started to desire things other people had because I felt as though it would give me status and admiration. Many people do the same thing in their lives. They fail to realize that if all they can be are things they are connected to, then they have lost the essence of who they are.

I preach and advocate for people to understand and identify who they are as an individual. There is nothing wrong with admiring the accomplishments of someone else, or even modeling the path and lifestyle of someone else as it relates to yours, BUT you need to be able to come into your own. This is one of the main reasons why people get disappointed in life. Many adopt a position where they feel if they do not have what those who they emulate have, they are not adequate or accomplished. Just like you cannot walk in anyone else's shoes, you should not view life through someone else's lens. When I look at my mentors, leaders, heroes and sheroes I do not want to acquire what they have acquired. I would like to thank the great men who wrote the forwards to this book. All three are great leaders and positive mentors in my life. The only thing I desire from them is the knowledge and wisdom they used in order to be successful. I refuse to read of the successes of someone else without creating a blue print for my own!

Destiny mentality will always place you in a position to receive and not just believe.

There is this idea circulating the world and people about the law of attraction. As I understand and practice it, it works with the law of physics and energy. You must be able to view yourself as a cosmic magnet. The positive energy you put out into the universe will reciprocate itself for you in positive things and enjoyments of life. As I have shared this information and have studied this law I have come to realize that many confuse the law of attraction with wishful thinking and positive believing. In the next section I speak about faith and works. I propose to you that a person who only believes will find themselves in a magic show; never fully gaining from the reality of life. Life is more than just believing.

Experiencing life is more than just about wishful thinking and happy thoughts. Your greatest desire should always be in a position to receive what God has in store for you. I found joy in my life when I began to put my dreams into action and actually began to seek after the harvest from the seeds I had planted. When I began being passionate about my work, favor and life began to open endless possibilities for success and favor. I want you to get to the position where your greatest desire is to watch what you imagine come to life in front of your eyes!

Developing a destiny mentality takes focus, faith, and favor.

These three Fs are the building blocks to becoming successful in the adventure we call life. It is my goal to outline what these traits are, why they are important to your venture and how to identify them in your life. One of the issues many face is overcoming the stumbling blocks of life. With these blocks you must be able to work with the three F's. Understand that two of these concepts are controllable and manageable (Focus and Faith). Favor, on the other hand, is something you learn to position yourself to receive. You cannot control favor when it falls, but you can control your position when favor is falling in your environment. These three elements are things you need to be able to identify and work together for your good. You need to understand their importance in your life. You also need to recognize these keys can be mastered when administered correctly. Before you continue I encourage you to put aside your previous thoughts and definitions about these words. Open your mind to a new awareness of these concepts as they relate to your destiny.

Focus in the sense of seeing the vision. Many people view focus through a very narrow lens. Focus does not mean, in the context of this book, staring aimlessly at a dream board and creating mental pictures to reference as you go throughout the day. I want you to view focus as putting on your vision glasses and zoning in on clues and things in your environment that point you in the direction of your destiny. I challenge you not to focus on things you want, but rather the path. Focus on things that will get you to where you have to go. The conflict that many face is they spend too much time focusing on the dream, and never setting forth the vision. Focus tends to be on the tangible things of life you seek to obtain. However I challenge you to a position your eyes on the road that will lead you to where you gave to go. When I say focus on vision that is exactly what I mean. Do not focus on the outcome of the vision, but rather the totality of the vision and all its inner workings.

One thing I have been complimented on is being an extraordinary visionary. The thing that separates me from a person who just sees the vision is that I do the second part of scripture… I make it plain. Do not make your vision for life complicated. In my plain I focus on the plan. Many individuals focus on things and never focus on what they have to do in order to get those things done. I said to myself I wanted to live a successful life. I set vision for a certain type of lifestyle, with certain possessions and liberties. I did not stop at seeing the promise, but visioned a plan to make it happen.

For over three years I focused on writing a book. I saw it in my head, but for three years never put any words on a piece of paper. This is why many things in life do not work. You fall in love with the idea of it, but never make it real in your life. In order for you to move to the next level in your destiny quest you MUST move with the vision. Do not settle with the idea of owning a business… do it! Do not settle with the idea of going back and finishing school… do it! Do not settle with the idea of love… fall in love without recourse! Do not settle for the dreams… obtain the destiny! All these things are possible if you focus on the vision that God has given you.

Faith in the sense that destiny is obtainable. I am going to say something that may make some people cringe. I only intend to open your mind to a new realization of what faith is. Get to a place where you do not just have faith in the entity that is going to bring life into your existence, but rather

I challenge your faith to go to a level of believing that whatever you ask God for can be obtained. Many people have faith in God, or some higher being. My challenge throughout the years has always been trusting in God then not believing what I asked for can be done. How often do you pray for things to happen in your life? You have the "faith" that the creative force (God) will provide for you, but then at the end of your prayer you still operate out of fear and complacency; wondering if it will happen at all.

I challenge you, as you embark on this new journey of life, not only have faith in God, but have faith that God will do it. My elders would say when you pray, you should not worry… and if you worry, there is no point in praying. Studying the definitions of faith, there is one consistency; the element of the unknown. Persons get caught up in the "unknown" and forget what they do know…that all things are possible with God. As you operate in faith, know and understand that in your asking and in your work, that ALL things are possible. There is a reason I highlight the word ALL. Some people think I am crazy, but I believe with focus, faith, favor and work anything you put your mind to, actions to, being too is definitely possible. I came to this realization a long time ago when I began my destiny quest. I did not realize the reason I was not accomplishing things in my life was because I did not believe I could be nor could have it. I looked at my family background. I look at my education level. I looked at the community I was raised in and said to myself,

"Can no good come out of Baltimore?" Then I started to look at the lives of other successful persons and realized some of them had it harder than I did! You should appreciate you have been given the same potential as other great persons in our history. The question becomes if your faith causes you to believe you have more than enough ingredients for the recipe of success.

Favor in the sense of divine intervention and assistance. We all need help. In our quest to obtain what God has for us, understand that it is neither your power nor your potential that creates. Only what God favors in your life. Learn to depend on the creator of sources. Know that it is only through this creativity that things can come to pass. Many people lack favor in their lives because: 1) They do not acknowledge the need for the creator or 2) they have not built a relationship with the creator to where favor can be shown in their lives. Another thing to take into consideration with favor is that you have to be in the right position in order to receive it. (I hope that you are catching the underline message in this book.☺)

As I talk to individuals about life and the struggles associated with moving towards their goals I hear a consistent mantra: "Why is life such a struggle?" & "Why don't things come to me like they do for others?" Favor appears to operate in a mysterious manner.

Turn Your Dreams Into Destiny!	
What You Dream?	**How to Create Destiny?**

In the chart above list things in your life you find yourself dreaming about. In the space provided next to it write a plan on how you plan on accomplishing this dream.

CHAPTER 2

Your Destin-ography

Reading your lines

Every story has a script. Persons forget that their story has already been written out for them. Your main goal and objective is to follow the script. I stress the importance of studying and reading the script of your life. Understand the promises associated with the script. I meet individuals who speak about fulfilling destiny but do not know the promises associated with destiny. The best way to obtain the promises of God is to read His word back to Him. I stress the importance and relevance of literally telling God what God has said.

There are two things I want to address in this chapter; 1) Knowing Gods plan for your life and, 2) Being able to know and articulate what your plan in life needs to be. You will have a clearer picture of where you are going in life when you write it down. It is important to refer to the scripture that says, *"And the LORD answered me, and said, Write the vision, and make it plain upon tables, that he may run that readeth it."* Many people go through life with no clear direction. They have no clear direction because they have not written a plan or course of action. Understanding your script is important as you continue to go through life.

I want to address the issue of creating and knowing what your plan is. I want to go into uncovering and understanding what God's will is for your life. How often do you find yourself waking up in the morning and telling yourself the things you need to do? However, by the time you get to the end of the day you only have a portion of those tasks accomplished. Some people create a "to do" list that's followed through the day. You wake up in the morning, grab the pad next to your bed, and make a list of all the things you need to get accomplished. You figure out how they are going to operate and in what sequence. We have progressed to the age in our lives were, like I do, we just refer to our blackberry or iphone to tell us what to do. But how many of you administer the same type of structure and planning for your life? The problem with many people is they plan their life on a day by day basis. The farthest many will go in serious planning is a week. Very seldom do we plan for longevity. I challenge you to organize your life to the best of your ability.

See the bigger picture in your life and then be able to plan for that event to manifest itself in your life. There is no point in saying you want destiny (life long process) to unfold when you are planning using a daily to-do list. You must be able to see the vision and have the ability to set forth the vision. Look at what the universe is drawing you toward. Then make sure the vision becomes manifested, at least, on paper. There is a reason the bible is so adamant about writing the vision. This is the first realization of what happens in your mind can become manifested in your reality. I encourage you to write your story before you even begin. Many stories are written after they are done. Why wait for someone else to write your story, when you can write it and then tweak it as you go?

I am sure many of you are asking the great question of life "How do I know what God has for me?" There are two things to keep in mind:

1) Destiny is consistent, purpose is not.

2) God will never totally reveal the entire picture.

So often do people confuse their purpose with their destiny. There is a difference between the two. Purpose is what God wants you to do in a particular span of time. God will always allow you to operate with purpose, dependent on the environment you are called to serve in. As societies change and as your environment changes, so will your purpose in these situations. Destiny on the other hand will encompass the totality of your purposes over the course of your existence. In trying to uncover and know what God has in store for your life and how to operate in it, I encourage you to use something I would like to identify as the "Call Meter".

We are consistently being drawn toward destiny. Anything you feel a pull towards will more than likely be in line with your destiny. Anything you find yourself struggling against is more than likely not in line with your call meter. It is not a matter of listening for the voice of God, as much as it is keeping your eyes open for opportunities that draw you towards success and greatness. Making sure your spirit, emotions and will are aligned with one another. This will assist you in carrying out the purposes that will lead you toward your destiny.

Adapting to your environments

The main indicators to receive the blessings of God are to be placed in the right position, in the right environment and at the right time. Understand your environments will consistently change. Along with these changing environments you must adapt to the season you are drawn into. You only remain in certain environments until you learn the lesson or complete the task assigned. Then you are able to move forward to the next level. There is nothing more detrimental than staying in the same place for too long, moving to the next level unprepared or dwelling in the past.

1) Staying in a place for too long can pose two major effects. The first being you get comfortable at a level you have already outgrown. At the same extent you run the risk of missing opportunities that only come around once. You spend the rest of your life playing catch up.

2) Moving to the next level prematurely will cause you to be unprepared to operate fully in your potential. There are people who attempt to "get there", but never learned what they "got here". God wants you to be progressive. But God also wants you to do it in a timing that will not set you up for failure. You must bring the right tools and knowledge along with you.

3) Many people dwell in the past. I am not referencing what others refer to as living with the experiences of your past looming over your shoulder. I write in reference to the majority people who drive their cars looking in the rear view mirror. Use your past as a point of reference, but make your inspiration come from your current consciousness. Do this in light of the context you have been placed in and not your past memory from a situation you use to be in. Learning to adapt and being able to flow with your environment is a very important skill to master as you go on your destiny quest.

Interacting with characters

You were created to build relationships. How your story progresses is contingent on your interactions with those you come in contact with in your journey. Although you are the leading character in your story there will be individuals in your life that will be there for a purpose and a season. Do not let anyone steal your shine and do not let "extras" stay in your story for too long. People play a pivotal role in your story; but as you interact with them, you are playing an important role in their story. We have lost the importance of relationships. Keep in mind I am not talking about intimate relationships you would build with your partner. Nor am I referring to the type of relationships you build with a family member or friend. When I speak of relationships I speak to how we interact with humanity and our environment as a whole.

There is no need in functioning with society if you cannot build a connection with the community you are a part of. People have become selfish and stubborn in the sense that they have more concern for their bubble; instead of taking into consideration the great "bubble" of life we call earth. When I was doing my undergraduate and graduate work I realized that students are the loneliest persons in our society. One would think with all the cultures, people and interactions that take place; persons would be able to build relationships with one another. How many times do you talk to, or even smile at a perfect stranger walking along the street? You interact with so many hurting people on a daily basis and do not even know they are hurting. How you interact with others will determine how humanity interacts with others. People look at me as if I am crazy when I tell them about my interactions and dialogue with persons from other religions, cultures and ethnicities. My philosophy is we all have things we can learn from one another. There is a reason divided people has hindered the progress of the world. I vision a day where we can live, marry, econ, worship and work with one another; to do this and still be able to function normally with our differences. We all have a commonality. We are all human. Just dwell on what it means to be a human being. Appreciate the autonomous nature of human beings. Do this and we will be able to function communally. Who cares what you call your God? Who cares how you cook your food? Who cares what language you speak? The only thing we should be concerned about is having love for all humans who were placed on this planet to fulfill purpose and destiny.

Playing the cards dealt

You have no control over what the universe decides to do with your life. You do have control over your perception of the cards dealt to you. In Gods eyes everything that happens is neither good nor bad, but they are for a reason. It is your perception about the situation that makes it good or bad. I will never forget my first poker tournament in Las Vegas. Out of 100+ players I made it to the top 15 by playing less than 20 hands. I learned from the song that you have to "know when to hold them and know when to fold them". The same concept applies to your life. Your attitude and energy about a situation will determine the outcome. Realty is stuff happens. If you focus on the wrapping paper alone you will miss out on the reality that the gift, lesson, and opportunity still needs to be uncovered. As I get into the next chapters I will discuss more specifically on how to handle certain aspects of life. I want to dialogue with you on accepting reality for what it is. Use your reality as the tool needed to get to the next level. My dad, before retiring, was a construction worker. He knows everything there is to know about building, welding, beams and windows. Although the gift of building did not transfer to me, there is one thing I learned from my father. Learn how to use the tools in front of you. I do not care what you need to accomplish in life, there are things around you that can be used for your good. You must become the Inspector Gadget of your own adventure.

When faced with a problem, dilemma, or obstacle learn to use what you have. When potential and creativity meet, a solution for any problem can be made. I encourage you to take what you have and appreciate it. Then ask God to show you the need for those things in your life. The reason many people lose out on opportunities and progression is because God gives them what they need but do nothing with it. Stewardship is important. Wherever you are in life, you have been given the tools needed to accomplish the task you have been set out to achieve. I get exhausted listening to people say they do not have what they need in order to be successful. God will never bless you with anything if you do not learn how to use and appreciate what you have. Get to a place in life where whether you are dealt a "positive" hand or a "hard to play" hand… make sure you do something with it! With some hands there is nothing you can do but "fold em'" as they say in poker. But with regards to your life, God will honor those who let go and let God. God is looking for those who are given a "good hand" and will play it with wisdom, knowledge and gusto. At the same time, God is looking for those who are given a "hard to play hand" and will play it with wisdom, knowledge and gusto.

Role playing

As the leading character there is not only one role you play in life but multiple roles and personalities based on environments, situations and interactions with other characters. There is a mis-identity in your story because you do not know how to balance the roles you are supposed to fill. God calls for balance in our lives. Learning how to multi-role is important in playing an award winning character. There is nothing worse than not knowing who you are and the role you are intended to play. You can not confuse your roles and you should not pull out the wrong hat in the wrong environment.

There is an exercise I want you do. Say your name. Since I know the majority of you just said your first name, I want you to say your full name. If there are any titles, say your name with your titles (i.e. Dr., attorney, pastor, teacher, manager). I think we can take this a step further. I want you to say your name with all the roles you fill. Do not just call out the main ones. Do your best to name everything you become in the course of the day. Say who you are to your environments and the people around you. Do you see and understand the multiple roles you play throughout the course of your day. Be real with yourself and identify times throughout the day where you either mix your roles or are unsure what role you are suppose to be playing. It can be psychologically confusing knowing who you are as it relates to the many roles you have been called to play.

My encouragement is that you look deep within to see who you are. Do not get confused with identifying yourself with the roles you play. One thing I have learned is that God has not called you to do anything in life. We get so caught up in doing and acting that we lose the true essence of creating. Know that God has called you to be something. It is in the process of doing that you become what you have been called to be. A role is an opportunity to portray a particular persona, during a given time, in order to relay a message of influence in a particular context or environment. Ask God the same question an actor/actress would ask the director; "What's my motivation?" The response you get from God will determine the role you play in route to living out your destiny.

Preparing for the every changing plot

Being unprepared is just as bad as being unequipped. There are preventative and preparative things you must be aware of as you embark on your journey. You must understand the differences between the punctuations in your life. Know when and how to label them. When you do not know where you are (point of departure) it is hard to set up where you are going (point of destination). Learn how to position yourself for change. Change is very difficult for a lot of people to deal with. In this chapter I do not wish to focus on the downside of change, but rather offer a more enlightening lens on what change is as it relates to your path of destiny.

WOMEN- Think about the last time you changed your purse. It may have been this month, this week, today, or even 3-4 times today! Ask yourself the question why? Why do you feel the need to remove all your belongings from one bag and place them in another? Is it because you needed a smaller purse than you did yesterday? Is it because yesterday's purse does not match today's outfit? Or maybe you know the compliments you get on the selected bag will be your confidence booster for the day?

MEN- Think about the last time you changed the sporting team you support. (WOW that was hard to think of given the fact that men do not change much of anything). Ask yourself the question why? Why is it that after spending thousands of dollars in regalia you would switch in the short time between seasons? Did the team you support not play well in the past season so you decided to go with a stronger team this season? Did your previous team lose one of their key players and you decided to the support the player's new team instead of the old? Or maybe you have come to the realization the team you

have supported for many years are not championship
material?

The point I want to make is changes happen and
there are many different influences on why we are compelled
to change. I am encouraging you to embrace change because
I know you do not want to remain the same. I want you to
embrace change because in order for you to get to where you
are going you can not arrive as the person you are. Your
environments are always, and will always be, consistently
changing. Understand there is a constant pressing for change.
You are pressed externally by your environments. I encourage
you to be pressed internally by the call for change from your
inner man. The best way to prepare for change is very simple:
know it is coming! There is no set way or strategy I can tell
you that will help you prepare for change. I can encourage
you to keep in the forefront of your consciousness that
change WILL come. The reason many do not do well with
change is because "they didn't see it coming". So when
change does come, not only are they unequipped, but they are
also unprepared. One thing I learned in driving school was
how to drive defensively. You may not be aware of what
other cars are going to do around you, but you need to always
be prepared for some knuckle head to make a move that will
put you in a ditch! Be aware of your environment, and open
to the impression that your environment is making on you.

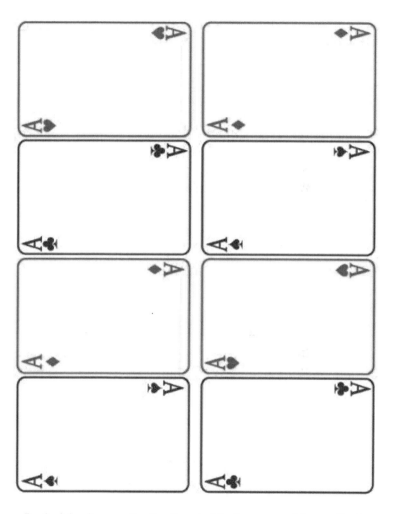

In the left column write situations in life that are troublesome. In the right column write the new perspective you will have about the issue.

CHAPTER 3

Understanding The Need for Punctuations:

Life was not intended to be predictable

Do you really want to know?

When I talk to individuals they express concerns about knowing. Then I ask them if they really want to know? I have gotten to a position where I would care not to know. Knowing creates two types of situations.

1.) When you do not know, faith is tested. One of the key elements to faith, as stated in the previous chapter, is the unknown or the unclear. I am amazed at people who claim and profess to have faith; however they are always inquiring the ins and outs of a given situation.

My father use to tell me "no news is good news". I have adopted that idea to a lot of things I do. There was a time in life where I wanted to know and uncover the mysteries of God. Now I have gotten to a position where God's mysteriousness becomes my motivation to seek after Him. I must reiterate that life is not, and was not, intended to be predictable. Think about it in this light; the more you know, the less faith you need to employ in any given situation.

Knowing can become a handicap for your faith. I challenge you to get to a position in life where your faith stands on its own; without the crutches of knowing and fear. Learn to breakthrough your situation, not with your mind (knowing) but, through your faith (trust in God). When trouble and obstacles arise try not to figure out the solution through your knowledge. But allow God to work it out through your faith.

2.) When you do know you run the risk of projecting your influence in the process of the outcome.

Be real with yourself. The more you know about something the more you try to influence it. Have you ever noticed the second you find out about an event or an occurrence in your life (wedding, anniversary, graduation, pregnancy) this is also the moment you decide the amount of influence and things you will do surrounding the event? People do the same thing with Gods will in their lives. I find it amazing how people can receive a portion of the word, and before God is done giving instruction have already imposed what they want to take place. This is very dangerous in the fact that sometimes, God does not want us to get involved in the process. Rather you should let God be God. It is very dangerous working with God. I am reminded of a poem I spoke in elementary school that is true to our everyday situations. The author is unknown-

"As children bring their broken toys with tears for us to mend,

I brought my broken dreams to God because He was my friend.

But then instead of leaving Him in peace to work alone,

I hung around and tried to help in ways that were my own.

At last I snatched them back and cried, how can you be so slow?

My child, he said, what more could I do, you never did let go!"

Many have a "hold on" mentality when it comes to working with God. Instead of working with God, God becomes staggered in His progress because He ends up having to work with us! If God showed us the end result of some things, it would blow our minds. There are some things God will reveal to you only in the spirit. The reason He reveals it in the spirit is because if He revealed it in the natural you may not be prepared for it. Accept the fact that whatever happens happens. To know why is not important.

Life is always changing and evolving

Understand the need for change. I would hate to live an existence that was never evolving. It is interesting people who say they want to change but do not want to let the change take place. There is no point in asking for change and then fighting against the things that must evolve, be added, or deleted in order to make change happen. A fight against change is a fight against progress. Think about some things you can visibly see that you have changed in your life. Maybe you have changed addresses. You have changed a hairstyle. You have changed jobs or careers. You have changed a goal or vision in your life. You have changed your furniture around a couple of times. You have changed cars. You have changed friends and relationships. But there is a challenge about change and transformation. With external changes, there should be an internal change and evolution taking place as well. There is no need for your environment and external self to change when you remain the same person on the inside. Learn to view change, not as the enemy, but as the agent by which true transformation can take place.

There are many people in this world still in the place they are because they refuse to move with time. Think about it…they are in a marriage, but still view relationships as they did in High School. They got a promotion, but still have the "stand over my shoulder and tell me what to do" work ethic. They are making more money because of the business they started, but still have the same spending habits. They go to church on a weekly basis, but there is no compassion for their fellow person. Maybe one of these examples sounds familiar to you? My point is their environment has changed, but they have not. We get afraid of change because we do not realize that change is a process needed for transformation.

Understand the difference between change and transformation as they relate to your life and your destiny. Change is something that can always be reversed, undone, or redone another way. Look at the list I shared with you earlier about things we change in our lives. Every change scenario you can think of can be undone, redone, or reversed. But when transformation takes place the end result is nothing close to the beginning. When it comes to change and transformation you compile the changes you are making and use them as the building blocks for your transformation.

Time is moving forward... are you moving with it?

You cannot stop time from moving forward. You can stop yourself from moving forward. When we look at our lives through the lens of the present we can never be prepared for what lies in our future. It is like going to the eye doctor; when your vision changes so must the lens change too. I hate to see people get left behind. Take a look back on your life and identify situations and people you have left behind. Identify people and situations in your life you need to leave behind now. I remember growing up and being told there is a time where as you are climbing up the ladder of life there will be people you may have to go back down and help bring up with you. I am not negating and saying to do away with this concept of love; however I do believe everyone is not meant to go to the next level with you. Certain individuals may start at the bottom of the ladder with you, but their destination/top is different than yours.

You cannot be afraid to move and take action when the world is literally moving under your feet. Every day God is looking for people who will seize every moment as an opportunity to create from the unlimited potential we are presented. There is a reason your time clock has been synchronized with the watch of the universe. The moment you came to planet earth was a specific time. In between this time and your expiration date is what you will be held responsible for when you stand before the creator.

The only thing hindering your progress is not only you… but your action. Action is pivotal in progression. As I stated earlier in this chapter, many things are moving around you, seen and unseen. Realization comes when you look around and see everything moving, however you are still staying in the same place. There was a point in my life where I had an "aha!" moment. There was a time where everyone and everything around me was progressing and doing well. People were getting degrees, producing albums, starting new businesses, running organizations, getting new jobs and promotions, and what was I doing? Watching! Some of you are living in an environment where people around you are progressing and being blessed. You are wondering what the issue is? The issue is that you are not taking action. The issue is that you are not taking advantage of the potential and fruitful environment you are in. If there are positive things and positive energy around you, you should be able to tap into that force and begin to co-create with the universe your own happiness. If there are other surfers around you and they are catching good waves, learn to ride one when it comes. Time is always acting; it is moving forward. The question is you moving with it?

Living a life of Adventure

Your life is not a sitcom, commercial or short film. Life is a continuation of multiple story lines connected to the same character. When you view life as an adventure your focus is always on obtaining and finding the treasure chest. It does not matter how many moots you must cross, dragons you must slay or princesses you must save. When I look at the great adventure God has set before me I only see each element of life as bringing me one step closer to my treasure. You must get to the point where you are consciously moving towards something.

I have never been a big fan of adventure movies or novels about faraway lands. I am a fan of a good personal adventure. Go back in your childhood. Remember the days where you would get a table, a few chairs, a blanket, and some pillows and you created your own fort or house? Remember when you would go outside and there was some tree in the woods you would see from a distance? You made it your personal quest to battle the forest monsters, and the mole people in order to get to the tree? Remember how your parents saw a milk carton; but you saw a car, a boat, a plane or a basketball hoop☺? Remember entering the hallowed halls of the institution of choice? The only thing you saw was a degree at the end of your term. You understood the adventure and challenges involved in obtaining your goal? Remember when anxiety of the proposal happened? His hands were sweating. Your eyes began to water. You then realized at some point the lifelong commitment to share your life adventure with someone else? Remember the day you decided to make a spiritual commitment to live a good, moral and ethical life? Then you realized you had a long way to go and a lot to do?

Life is a process. Not only is it a process, but it is a systematic, well thought out, predetermined course of events and situations all taking place in the context of multiple environments. Life gives you a call to act in your holistic self. There is also the call for you to act multidimensional in order to get to the place (achieved goals) the universe has planned for you. You will never be "over" with life. When you are done with one scene, the saga continues into something else. Never view a situation in your life as your ultimate demise. Remember "what the caterpillar views as the end of the world… the master calls a butterfly".

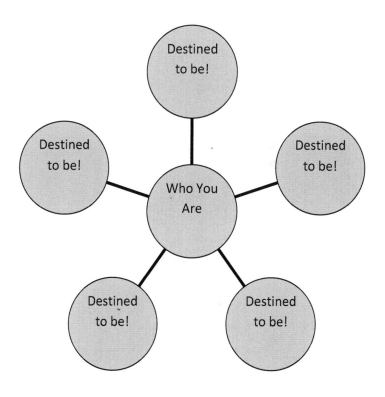

In the diagram above write your name and the roles you play in the center. In the circles surrounding write what you believe God is calling you to be/become.

CHAPTER 4

Understanding the ? (Question Marks) of life:

When you find yourself asking God questions

Why things do not work?

One of the questions we ask God is why. Why after hard work and effort, things do not occur the way you intended for them to be? There are two things to assist in understanding the answer to this question. God will never place you in a position until you are ready to handle it. The reason things do not work in your life is because God does not want them to. I do not want you to think God is holding things back from you because He is mean. I do not want you to think it is some cruel punishment for your sins; or your faith for that matter. Rather think of it as a deposit hold. Working at a bank, one of the most difficult things you can hear from the banker, and tell a customer, is that there will be a delay of funds availability. There are two main reasons why a person would have a delay of funds on a deposit to their account. Either they have overdrawn there account numerous times and the bank wants to ensure the funds before giving it to the customer to splurge. Or the deposit is outside the norm for the customer and does not line up with the customer's account history. Either way, God works in the same manner. God will never place you in a position to receive until God's wisdom sees fit for you to receive it. You must learn to trust the wisdom of God over your knowledge.

Secondarily, your perception and predicted outcome is not always what you think it will be. With that in mind, God protects you by not allowing some things to work out for you. There is a reason I love Ephesians 3:20.

"Now unto him that is able to do exceeding abundantly above all that we ask or think, according to the power that worketh in us,"

Think about it. How many times are the results you asked for exactly what you wanted? You may have wanted the situation to be one way, but God turned it around and gave you something you were never expecting. I am reminded of the story about a man who prayed for $100,000. After hard work and much success he received $97,000 instead. Do you think he complained? I have learned that either way God chooses to bless me, a blessing is a blessing, regardless of the size or when it comes! Some things do not work well because we do not always do the necessary things to make them work. Your plan is not always the right plan to make things happen.

Why things do not happen?

This question is very similar to the question posed in the previous chapter. Understand the difference between things working for you and things happening for you. When I talk about things working for your good this implies there is some mechanism or system in place orchestrating an end result. For an engine to work, there are many different parts that must function at the same time. In order for a relationship to work it takes the collaborative effort of all parties in order to compromise and be flexible. In order for an organization to work, it takes the parts and inputs of all employees in order to keep the machine running. In order for God to work things in your life, God has to orchestrate them. God will position things in the right place and at the right time. The compromise is that you be in the right place at the right time.

Happenings are completely different. When things happen, it is not to say there was not a system involved however, there is no need for a logical explanation. Think about it in these regards; when you happened to get the job, it was favor that made it happen. When you happened to find the right partner to spend your life with, it was destiny that had you join up from half way around the world. When your business happened to land the contract over all the other bids, it was favor that got you to that position. When the sickness happened to have gone away, trust me, there was no logical explanation that was needed. Understand when you do not see a thing happening in your life it is not because the work isn't being done. Rather know that happenings are out of your control. You can control the work you do in order to get where you are trying to go. However there is no way you can control results (happenings). Results are the product of your actions, but happenings are the products of Gods influence on your actions. Things do not just happen without the influence of God. Desire that God you not only produce results in your life, but you desire God to get involved in your happenings. Happenings occur as a direct result of God getting involved in your work. So to answer the original question, things do not happen because we do not allow God to get involved. Many are busy with the idea that their work is going to be enough. When you find yourself asking these intricate questions analyze if you are allowing God to do His work with you. Allow me to reiterate the differences. Things work because of the mechanisms associated with them. Things do not happen because people do not allow the influence of God in their lives.

Example 1: A car does not work because the radiator (mechanism) is not functioning correctly. It will continue to remain broke until the car is taken to the repair shop. In order to get results, your energy (happening) has to collaborate with the repair man (God) in order to work out a solution. Do not leave life in the garage waiting for it to fix itself. Your actions must meet God's favor.

The motive of an inquiring actor

There is no problem with asking questions. I have never understood why some people say you should not ask God questions. I have come to the conclusion that persons who say this have no clear direction for where they are going in life. I would also like to make the assumption that they have no intimate relationship with God. When you ask questions you are letting the person know you are looking for clarity. All questions asked are not questions used to be belligerent. Rather we use questions to get clarity, gain information and create dialogue. One thing I was always told in school was there is no such thing as a stupid question. The only stupid question is the one you do not ask.

You should have a relationship with God where you can ask clarifying questions. You should be able to get information from God. You should feel comfortable creating dialogue with God. Get outside the idea that God is so far away and impersonal that He does not want to have anything to do with you. Many are afraid to ask God questions because they are:

1.) Afraid of the response or

2.) Afraid of the response.

I can think of other reasons people do not like to question God, however, the main reason is when God begins to answer; it can be a very scary thing. When God speaks, if He so chooses to, He will always answer exactly what you asked. The other uneasy aspect of this is He will always tell the truth. This is an uncomfortable thing to consider when you begin inquiring about your destiny. If we answered questions the same way God answers questions, none of us would have any friends and we would remain upset and mad at one another. As much as we say we love truth, telling the truth is hard. Hearing the truth brings about another level of anxiety. The bible talks about making your petitions known before God, but it also makes reference to going to God for clarity and direction. Life can be best explained to us if we ask God clarifying questions.

Some questions are best left unanswered!

You do not have to know everything. Yes I am telling you to be inquisitive with God about things that are happening in your world as it relates to your life. However, do not get to the position where you nag God about everything you do not know. The next time you go to church, or even find yourself praying, analyze the prayer to see if your motivation is to get answers or truly dialogue with God? Every question does not have a question mark at the end of the sentence. Some questions in our lives are best left implicit. In your conversations with God seek to build relationship. Make relationship through dialogue your core focus. Understand some things should remain undisclosed/ sacred from us. In the secrecy and mystery of God you will be challenged to seek more of Him, His Will and His Purpose for your life.

I would suggest you adopt an attitude of unexpectancy. If you do not know its coming you will appreciate blessings more when they arrive. **Women please**

consider this: It is your anniversary and your partner has something great planned for you. He has given hints and clues but you still have no idea what the actual plans are. The only thing you know is his love and affection will be brought out in his actions. **Men consider this:** The same anxious feeling arises when you call your partner at home telling her that you have had a long day at work. She replies, "I've got something special for you when you get home honey". Sometimes you need to allow the goodness and love of God to just happen in your life. He has already promised you great things are coming. He may have given you ideas and answers to your questions. Whatever it is, God has given you what He wants you to know. All you must do is wait and anticipate the great things coming your way.

Keep in mind our motives in asking will also determine how God/ if God will reveal things to us. You cannot handle some truths. If you were honest with yourself, you would admit you can be selfish and manipulative with your questions. Some things we do because there is a certain response we want to get from God. You must know regardless of what your lips and mind may say, God reads your heart. You have been requesting things from God on things your flesh desires. Ask yourself if you asking God questions from yourself or from your heart? Sometimes you will ask God a question thinking His response is going to be about someone or something else. In actuality His response, in most cases, will be focused towards you!

Preparing for the response.

There is often a waiting period between asking a question and receiving an answer. What should be happening in this process is preparation for the response. There is nothing worse than not being prepared for bad news or good news. The question becomes whether or not you are going to be content with the response or reactive to the response, whatever the case may be. Understand if you never find the reason, trust God it was there...

In the whitespace surrounding the clouds write questions you have about the areas surrounding your life. DO NOT CREATE ANSWERS! *In your meditations pray God would reveal these answers.*

CHAPTER 5

Understanding the ! (Exclamations) of life:

When you find yourself in drama

Drama that hurts

Hurt, pain and suffering are all natural occurrences of life. There is no way you can avoid drama. I do not care where you go, how good of a person you are, or what you have. Since you live in an imperfect world there are going to be things you go through that will not feel good. Please note a life without drama is an unrealistic expectancy. I try my hardest to understand why people get so bent out of shape when drama occurs? I try to fathom why they attempt to run from drama and separate themselves when they are a part of it. Have you ever noticed the person who always speaks about others who bring drama, hurt and pain are the main ones who are at the source of every problem? People who are constantly complaining about the storm in their lives are the main ones going through something? I use to date a young lady who was always going through something. She was always complaining. Not only was she complaining about her problems, but she would tell me about the craziness of everyone else's too! There was a point in our relationship where I hated picking up the phone. I knew the conversation would always be the same. "How was your day? How was work?" Then would come the laundry list of her and everyone else's problems.

It was intended for you to experience a little bit of drama in life. Hurt is actually healthy. It allows you to realize you are still human. Hurt also allows you to realize your emotions are in tack. Think about it in terms of biology. Your body communicates issues by way of an alarm of hurt. Some people are emotionally disconnected from themselves and from life. They became disconnected because they do not allow hurt to be the tool that brings them emotional balance. Men think they are invisible and bionic. Men assume hurt should not affect them and emotional disconnectivity is the best way to handle it. Persons who do not allow themselves to hurt will never have the opportunity to heal. I pity the individual who wants everything to be easy. When you go through drama your faith is increased. True faith is not about how you handle the roses and butterflies in life, however, true faith is tested when you can look drama in the face and say, "Tho He slay me... yet will I trust Him"! You would not be the person of faith you are today, if you did not experience some hell and high water. You would not be the go getter you are today if a little fire were not placed under you to get you going. You would not know what true love was if you did not go through some knuckleheads in your life. You could not appreciate a personal walk or relationship with God if you did not experience the drama of the church. Get to a place where you welcome drama. For those who talk about you and attempt to make your life difficult, welcome them. These are the people who will help strengthen your faith.

You cannot be consumed by hurt. When you hurt or have drama I encourage you to experience it. Do not try to hide from the experience of drama. Do not dwell in it, but be in the moment God has placed you in. There is a reason you experience drama. There is a purpose you must fulfill, and drama is a part of your faith/destiny journey. I am not suggesting you run to drama for the sake of being in it. However, if you look up one day and find yourself in a situation you know will bring you heart aches and pain, thank God for the opportunity and experience it! Do not go and find the closest hole to bury your head in. Do not call your closest friend and make a big fuss about it. Instead find the closest secret closet and ask for direction on how to handle and get through the situation. Be sad! Cry! Get angry! Slap somebody if you need to! (Just kidding! I do not promote violence!). But whatever you do, do not dwell in those emotions. Do not allow them to take charge over you. If God did not intend for you to feel hurt or drama He would not have placed it in your life. Nor would He have equipped you with the emotions to feel the way you do.

Drama that opens your eyes

Sometimes God has to do drastic things in order to open up your eyes! It takes getting slapped around by life for God to show you His presence. Even as I am writing this book, there are literally hundreds of people around me going through drama. Because this book is being published nationwide, I cannot share details of people who have confided in my practice and ministry. However, I can assure you, we are all going through. The amazing thing I find consistent with people is that the problem they are facing is not the first time they have faced it. This is not the first time they have become pregnant. This is not the first time they have been late on their rent. This is not the first time they have run into trouble with the law. This is not the first time somebody made them mad. This is not the first instance they lost a job. This is not the first time they have experienced a broken heart. When you find yourself going through drama you have gone through before, realize God has you experiencing it again for a reason. In many cases it takes the experience of burning your hand on the stove to see the words of your parents were true. This is the same way God operates. Some do not build a relationship with God until an experience with God is forced upon them.

I have noticed in scripture sometimes God has to bring drama in your life in order to force a response out of you. I was shocked one day when I looked at multiple scriptures where God said that "He will MAKE us" do certain things. Two prominent scriptures are found in the book of Psalm and the Gospel According to Matthew. Psalm 23:2 says, *He will MAKE you lie down in green pastures.* The Gospel According to Matthew 4:19 says, *He will MAKE you fishers of men.* Could these scriptures suggest God will use force in our lives? Drama becomes good when God brings it into your life. Can you identify you became a better person when you came out of the dramas you were in? Learn that all experiences will work for your good. It is up to you to change your perspective about the situation. Sometimes the sound of the gun does people no good. Some persons need to feel the heated metal of the bullet to understand pain.

Look at the drama you are experiencing in your life. Ask yourself the question, "Does God have my attention?" We look at drama and situations for what they are. Many people never see the God inside the drama. Learn how to see God in the single parent experience. Learn how to see God in the prison cell. Learn how to see God in the bills piling up on the kitchen table. Learn how to see God in the broken relationship. With the same importance, learn to see the lesson as well. When drama comes I encourage you not to get mad or upset. Tell God He has your attention. Then ask God what He wants from you. Apologize for being stubborn. Focus your attention on the message. Sometimes it takes a bull horn to go off in your midnight hour to remind you that you should not be sleeping. Instead of sleeping you should be up praying.

Drama that's internal

One consistency I find in my counseling and advising is people who deal with drama find the majority of their issues are from internal problems. Many times in our spiritual walk we focus solely on the drama we can see and others see. However for the next couple of pages I want to focus on things that disturb and hurt you on the inside. We live in a community of broken people. We walk pass them. We work with them. We live with them. We follow them. We educate them. We see their clothes. We see their hairstyles. We see their lifestyles. We see their careers. But do we see their problems. While focusing on others, do you see the issues in yourself?

One of the greatest killers in our society is the silent killer. We all have them. They are the dramas you do not publish about yourself. They are the issues you seldom like to share with others. Situations like finances, sexuality, substance and alcohol abuse and mental illnesses to name a few. These are dramas everyone deals with and cannot be avoided. I give you a great commission to be transparent. I do not want you to be transparent with anyone, until you are first transparent with yourself! As you do this exercise on transparency I do not want you to feel wrong, dirty, or guilty about the things you are going through internally. Appreciate it is a part of you. There was a time in my life where I thought my issues were literal demons in me. I would think to myself, "Wendel how can you have a call on your life, be anointed and have these issues?" For a time I was depressed and hurt that these issues were a part of me. I was, as some of you are; mad at God for placing these desires and intimate hurts in me. You may not understand why the thorn is in your flesh. Do acknowledge you are bleeding, and a bandage is not going to fix the issue! Internal problems need to be addressed with intimate and intrusive attention. The problem with many people is they try to place a bandage on a diagnosis and never address the underline issue.

Your career is not the issue; but confidence and motivation is the problem. Your relationship is not the issue; but fear of being alone is the problem. Your education is not the issue; but discipline is the problem. Your spirituality is not the issue; but humble submission is the problem. Everything that happens to you externally is determined by what you think, feel, project, and express internally. It is a hard and serious struggle for people to look at themselves in the mirror and be naked; but not ashamed. It is a struggle to say, "I have dramas and here is what they are".

Many prefer to hide behind their successes and materialistic things. What they do not realize is these things do not aid in developing who they are holistically. You must be bold enough to, as my mentor Dr. Philip Dunston of Clark Atlanta University would say, "Chop your head off…turn it upside down…and look at the mess within". It is not going to be comfortable, nor a pretty sight, but knowing yourself is the first step to progress. You do not know who you are because you refuse to analyze who you are. As you are reading these pages understand the person you were five minutes ago is not the same person you are now. You may receive an email or call two minutes from now that will turn your life around. Your focus in life should not be about whom you are now, but rather the person the Potter is forming you into. The energy and drama God places around you are the mechanisms used to shape, mold and make you.

Your internal drama is used as a thermostat and not a thermometer. When faced with drama allow those things to set your pace and motivation. Do not allow them to dictate and tell you what you are. Often do we permit our internal issues to dictate the results of whom and what we are to become. We were created as emotional beings. Beings, who can emote, experience and balance internally and externally. In the next chapter I will identify the influences of our external problems. However, before we go there, we must take a look within. We must be able to take our silent issues as points of departure where we can cultivate change. We should not allow these issues to be the identifying factors for who we say we are.

Regardless of what you experience internally know a greater light outshines any internal issue. Learn how to tap into that light within. Learn to search for the light within. Learn how to find the light within. Beyond your issues is redemption. When you find yourself in compromising internal drama do not allow your emotions to set the atmosphere for your well being. Learn to acknowledge the internalized issue and use our spiritual thermostat to set the atmosphere.

Drama that is external

Sometimes life just gets hard. Understand you are a spiritual being having a human experience. You live in reality. The human experience is very hard to understand and comprehend. Every now and again you may ask yourself and God the question, what is the purpose of this carnal and physical experience? You rise daily and open our eyes, not into eternity, but into this world we call planet earth. You open your eyes and 98% of the things you experience are experienced through your senses. Be able to value that you live in a world where your physical body will have to go through some things in order to grow. My elders use to say if you live long enough sickness will come. Financial issues will arise. Partners will get on your last nerve. Employment will get funny. You will find yourself caught in a corner, between a rock and a hard place. You live in an existence where reality will be what it is...reality. My elders would also say "if you aint been through nothin'...keep livin'". The mere fact you are alive makes for the potential for you to experience external dramas.

Along with the human experience come the physical dramas of life. Sickness, poverty, loss of jobs, violence, hatred and genocide are all examples of things we face in our external environment. Be reminded things are not always as they seem on the level they are viewed. Although many things are unavoidable in your reality, get to a position where you do not allow external dramas to influence your spiritual progression. When I began a young adult ministry at my church I did some research on why young adults between the ages of 18-35 did not attend church. My discoveries were not astounding, but were consistent. The majority of studies focused on the fact that something external had happened in the individual's life that had cause them to stray from organized religion. There were examples such as work schedule, the death of a loved one, church drama, financial embarrassment, and partner perspectives. Another notation was since they were out of the house and under their parents rule they found no need to attend.

Think about external situations you have been through that have pulled you away from your spiritual walk. Maybe it was a traumatic event. Maybe you struggle with an addiction. Maybe it was a person who caused you to move you physical body in the opposite direction of where your spirit was calling you to go. Please know you will never get to a place of spiritual maturity, if you continue to allow flesh to control your destination. Getting to a place of "success" in your life does not guarantee spiritual safety, security, and growth. This is one of the reasons why many have external drama in their lives. There are situations God needs us to physically encounter in order to assist in the "crucifying of flesh" process. When you find yourself faced with external drama and uncomfortable situations know they are there in order to put your physical self in subject to the will of God.

If you were real with yourself you would admit you sometimes lose control of your actions. One question asked when we find ourselves in external drama is, 'how did I get here?' No wise person runs into external drama, nor wishes it upon their lives. But when we find ourselves in the situation we realize, at some point, we lost control. Yes, God does allow certain things to come about in our lives to experience. However, with relation to God's will and our free will, our choices and decisions are factors for why we experience. I have noticed people are quick to give blame to someone or something else, when what they need to learn is how to take responsibility for their outcomes. When you find yourself in a financial bind, bad relationship, bad career choice, or not at the level you want to be spiritually, learn to take responsibility for your portion of the outcome. The bills came and you decided to spend your money to get your hair or nails done. The partner you were with gave you the red flags they were unfaithful, but you allowed them to play you as a fool. You are out of right relationship with God because you refuse to seek after His will and His way.

When you learn to step outside your experience and view it from a distance you will be able to see the macrocosmic view of things. As long as you view things at eye level, you will never see nor understand the big picture.

There is a reason it is said all things happen for a reason. I would propose things not only happen for a reason, but "it" was "happening" before "it" got into your experience. "It" did not just pop into existence the first time you noticed it, but it was already in motion and being prepared to enter your experience before you knew anything about it.

When drama hinders destiny

Often we allow internal and external drama to hinder our lives and our path to acting out our destiny. You must be able to see how drama plays a disadvantageous role in your life. However, drama is necessary on your path towards destiny. While drama can and will come in your life, it should not hinder what God has set out for you to do. If you find drama hindering you from obtaining what the universe has predestined for you, do what you need to do in order to move forward. If you see drama has become an obstacle or a hindrance in your life, figure out a way to go around it, go under it, go over it, or breakthrough it. The problem with many is they experience drama, and will continue to experience drama, until they do something about it. I hope this next sentence does not offend anyone, but my elders use to say, "I don't want nobody peein' on me and telling me it's raining". Life is handing you things that are uncomfortable and hurtful; you are comfortable with it happening. You are comfortable being broke. You are comfortable in an unfulfilling relationship. You are comfortable at your job.

You are comfortable just going to church every Sunday. You are comfortable getting up every day and experiencing the same mess. If you were not, you would do something to change it. Make a decision in your life where you either live in the drama, or live to get through the drama. Do not be complacent, nor except the idea that drama is a natural condition.

I am reminded of being in grade school. There seemed to always be a fight after school. Those who would stay around to watch drama would always miss the bus going home. We do the same thing in our lives. Instead of allowing drama to be drama, we want to focus on it, watch it and become a part of it. Doing this causes us to miss the bus of life. How many opportunities have you missed because you were so focused on the bad going on in your life, that you were unable to see and appreciate the good? The reason your relationship ended the way it did was because you let the little dramas build up and never appreciated the little things. The reason you ended up in financial drama is because you would spend more time staring at your bills instead of staring at the "now hiring" sections of the newspaper. You have yet to experience the fullness of God because you are still concentrating on the time Ms. Mary said your attire was inappropriate for church. What external drama are you focused on, or apart of, that is holding you back? When drama hinders your destiny you may find yourself watching and hurting, instead of walking and healing. The best part of any movie is definitely the part with the most drama. But keep in mind you do have to get to the end of the story eventually.

Do not spazz out.... It is just part of the plot!

Many people overreact when drama comes! One question I ask as I look at the plight of others is "Why are they going crazy over the situation?" Now grant it, we all do it. We all have moments of insanity and positions of just losing our head. If you look at your life, how many times have you lost control of a situation because you lost control of yourself? You will be able to get through situations if you find moments to control yourself. A level head is the best starting point for planning and action. You will never be able to obtain your destiny, nor create a plan to handle your drama, if you are operating out of stress and anxiety. When drama arises in life you must learn to get a hold of the situation. But first you need to get a handle of yourself. It does a situation no good when you lose control. Many people are complacent with chaos. But know it is harder to manage chaos than it is to manage consistency. You can walk a clear path with drama around you. It takes you focusing on the path and not the environment the path has been placed in. I am reminded of the story of Dorothy in the *Wizard of Oz*. Regardless of the situations that arose in her quest to Oz, she never lost sight of the yellow brick road.

People assume I am crazy when I do not go wild about situations in my life. One word I learned from my mom growing up was the word "and". When we understand things happen and they are working out for our good, we will be able to see them in a different light. It is not developing an attitude of not caring. Rather you care enough about yourself not to stress yourself into an early grave. It is not that you are immune to drama, but when drama comes it has no effect on your immunity! It is not that you do not hurt, but when you get hit you know your healing is coming. You get to the point where you understand it is a part of the plot. So when bad news comes, do not get upset but say "and". Yes you got laid off …"and"? Yes the divorce happened… "and"? There is a fight after school… "and"…. "I GOT A BUS TO CATCH"! You cannot afford to get attached to drama to the point where you spazz out…. It is just a part of the plot! I learned from one of my father's in ministry that every time someone calls with drama does not mean I have to respond. This section is written to those who have a heart for service but find yourself being drug into other peoples drama. As my mentor would advise, some things can wait until the morning.

What Are You Fed Up With?

On the diagram above write things that make you upset. Feel the emotions as you write, but as you turn the page, leave these issues behind. Determine not to focus, but realize they have you emotionally oppressed!

CHAPTER 6

Understanding the . (Periods) of life:

Moving from chapter to chapter.

Understanding the concept of time

African philosophy teaches us time flows backwards. As your story unfolds, what has not happened is not a part of time. In other words you cannot give an account of situations that have not happened nor presented themselves yet. When you plan certain events to happen in your future you plan with faith that you will live to see that moment come to pass. In this chapter I seek to illustrate the need for understanding the concept of time and how it relates to your destiny. Over the course of history time has taken on many different lights. Time comes in the many formations of hours, minutes, seconds, days, years, seasons, moments and stillness. We have also seen the structure of time take many forms throughout history. The ways in which we tell time, and the duration of time has always been changing and evolving. I do not want to go into a history lesson on this topic, but rather would like to suggest your concept of time is different than others are reading these pages.

I challenge you not to think about time in the context or hours and minutes, but rather view time in the perspective of seasons and moments. Often we go throughout life with agendas and to-do lists. However many people never really live in the moment, nor understand the season, they are in. Before you begin delving in this chapter there is an exercise I would like to propose. If you are able to, as often as you can, DO NOT LOOK AT TIME. Have you noticed from the moment you arise, to the moment you close your eyes, you are focused on time? You open your eyes and, before you say thank you to God or good morning, you glance over to the clock to check the time. As you get in your car and turn the ignition you frequently glance at the time to make sure you will not be late for work. When you arrive to work you continuously check the time for two main events; lunch time and departure time. Even in your departure from work you check the time to make sure rush hour traffic will not hinder your path home. As you walk in the doors of you humble abode you check the time and plan dinner getting made, kids doing their homework, the football game coming on, or a special guest's arrival. As your evening comes to a close, you check the time in order make sure your day has been accomplished before you lay your body to finally rest. As you enter the bed, you glance one list time before your eyes close to unconsciousness to the same item you looked at when you woke up…the time.

My question, in light of this illustration, is how often do you step out of time and live in the moment and season God is allowing you to experience? Time is created not only to give you structure and organization, but to give the opportunity to place things in the right prospective. While you are focused on organizing the numbers of time throughout the day, how many times do you live without concern, or take in the power of creation around you? How you experience is contingent on the "time" you are in. Sleep is different to individuals depending on the time of day. Marriage and relationships can be different for individuals' dependant on the time of life they are living in. Financial troubles always seem to arise when there is a time of over debits and limited credits. Understand timing is everything! You cannot get caught up in things; time is of the essence.

Understanding the concept of moment

"Give me one moment in time. When I'm more than I thought I could be. When all of my dreams are a heartbeat away and the answers are all up to me. Give me one moment in time when I'm racing with destiny. Then in that one moment of time I will feel, I will be free."-
Whitney Houston (Moment in Time)

Moments are used as quick reminders of purpose. When the last time you experienced something and a moment was what helped you to appreciate it? As I experience my daily meditations I do not solely reflect on the happenings of my day. Rather I reflect on the moments I experienced throughout my day. Those moments where time was of least concern and I was truly being in my environment. I experience unplanned and unintentional moments where nothing is on my mind, but being. The amazing thing about these moments is I never plan them, nor do I realize I have experienced them until after the moment. Its times throughout the day where you come back to reality and realize for a moment you were in serene tranquility and peace. It is great to experience not just events in life, but the moments that come along with them.

Understand that moments of happiness are more valuable than the long eras of work that it took to get there. Look back on your life. You will see you have had more drama than happiness. However, the moments of happiness you experienced were most euphoric because of the drama you had to go through. There should be times in life where you realize how small you are in the great scheme of the universe. There should be times where you feel not only the heartbeat in your chest, but be able to hear the rhythm of life around you. Moments where you realize favor has been placed on your life. Moments where you have a feeling of genuine worth and accomplishment are important. There must be moments where love is not spoken nor felt, but committed to. There must be moments where fear becomes your motivator. There must be moments where you genuinely smile without reason; but just being alive.

Sometimes a moment is all you need. I remember growing up and my mother telling my siblings and me, "Give me a moment". Sometimes God will give you moments in order to remind you the promise is still obtainable.

Sometimes a glimpse of something is enough motivation to continue moving to the next level. To the same extent do not stay in the moment for a long period of time. Understand your seasons.

Understanding the concept of season

Seasons are not long. There is a reason for them being temporary. Certain experiences cannot happen momentarily because the lesson may be a bit more intricate. When you think about seasons you normally think about agriculture. It is necessary for seasons to occur for the purpose of things dying, being cultivated, growing, sprouting and things being harvested. Use this imagery when you think about the seasons in your life. There are periods and seasons you must go through in order for the cycle of life to take its course. Everything in this book could fall in the confines of your season. Understanding the season you are in and the purpose of that season are pivotal for your destiny growth and matriculation.

Seasons cannot happen forever. There are things you must leave behind in seasons in order to move on. As seasons progress, learn how to leave the seed behind and chase after the fruit. Many people lose the opportunity to harvest because they did not want to leave spring. They did not want to battle the heat of summer. They did not want to wait and be patient in fall. I challenge you to value the season you are in. Learn to plant seeds that are conducive to the season…then leave it behind. Get to a position where your seasons are recurrent and not permanent. As much as you wish summer could last forever, heat can become miserable. Appreciate that winter is needed for things to die. I challenge you to develop a sense of consciousness to your surroundings and seasons. I challenge you to appreciate the season you are in. I challenge you to appreciate all the seasons you are cycling through. Do not just be grateful for the harvest season. Thank God for the resources and the ability to plant in whatever season you are in. Note that every situation and experience you encounter is a seasonal occurrence. Very few things in life are meant to last forever. Just as seasons happen on a quarterly basis, the seasons in your life are a part of the great cycle. I constantly tell persons, God not only wants you to go around the mountain, God wants you to go up the mountain too. The only way He can do this is if He takes you through this cyclonic process.

The tragedy of dwelling in one scene for too long

There is nothing worse than watching a movie and having the same scene drug out for thirty minutes. However, there are certain things we allow to drag out in our lives. We allow marriages to drag themselves knowing the person we fell in love with is not the individual we sleep next to each night. We drag our jobs out knowing we can only get but so far up the corporate ladder. We stay in churches too long because we have developed a greater bond with the pastor than we have with God. We stay in our comfort zones for too long when God is calling us to go to the next level. There are periods in life that need to be opened, and some that need to be closed. However, they do not need to last forever. God gives you the will and control over periods in your life.

The amazing thing about periods is that you have the choice to dwell for a little while or get comfortable and set up camp. I want to address those of you who find yourself in the same experience for a long period. You have been in the place for so long, moving out for you is utterly scary and extremely uncomfortable. We all have times where we settle for complacency and mediocrity. We all have entered seasons or periods and gotten stuck before. There is a great travesty that occurs when we settle in one place for too long. I would like to use the illustration of frozen left-overs. My mother use to tell me some things just taste better later. You cook a meal (you). After partaking in it you decide you want to preserve it in the freezer (seasonal condition). Time begins to go by and you forget that the food (you) is still in the freezer (seasonal condition). Now, since you did not remove the food (you) out of the freezer (seasonal condition), what was meant to preserve you until you got better, now inflicts harm to you! Remind yourself of seasons in your life that were meant to preserve you and make you better. But because you wanted to stay in the comfort of the season you ended up getting burned! (This next sentence is a double negative but I must write it this way☺). Do not not get out of the freezer because it's cool. At some point God needs to remove you from the freezer and place you back on the oven.

Ending vs. transition

Things do cease to exist. Some things have to end. One of people's problems is they hold on to things that are meant to be let go of. They chase after things that do not want to be caught, nor meant to be caught. One of the hardest lessons I have learned in life is the process and law of detachment. Every now and again you need to do an inventory of things in your life. Go through the closet and garage of your inner being and see if there are things you need to depart from. What genuinely separates periods from the other points in this book is that periods do have a beginning and ending. We will always have questions. We will always experience drama. There will always be points of transformation and transition. However periods of life have a point of entry and a point of exit. You must stay in the mindset that whatever period you are experiencing, it is not the dictator to the outcome of your destiny.

I have gotten to a position in my ministry where I understand, and am excited, by the fact that what I am doing now will not last forever. Even as you have bought this book or have been given these pages, I realize that *"After the Comma"* will have to place a period in its moment of time. Regardless of what you are doing now, be comfortable knowing it will end one day. It is in the process of things ending that God can begin to set in motion something new. Do not confuse a situation being over with your destiny being over. View your situation being over as a transitional moment for destiny to continue. God is not putting a period in your life as an ending, but as the punctuation for your transition. Without the period the next sentence cannot begin. Without the period your life would be like a sentence; a run on with no definition or clear idea.

Letting go can be hard; especially when you find yourself coming to the end of one chapter in life. You cannot help but ask, "Does this really have to end?" I have spent many nights praying and crying because some chapters in my life I did not intend to end. At the same extent, I understand now that, some things have to end in order to properly transition. As a matter of fact I want some things to hurry up and blow over in my life now. Realize you cannot receive with hands clenched and holding... you have to let go.

Previous chapters are a point of reference and departure; not a place of welling

With the understanding that things happen in cycles, you know every ending can be viewed as a new beginning. With every passing of a test there is the preparation for a greater exam. All things that become old and die newness will eventually be born. One thing I encourage for you is not live in the past but rather use it as a place of exodus and a place of reference. I am reminded of many opportunities, good and bad, in my past where if I stayed I would not be where I am today. The problem with most people is when they look at their past they get caught up in the same emotions the past brought them. Instead of looking at broken relationships and fixing those problems uncovered in yourself, you decided sit on the couch with a picture of the person in one hand and a tub of ice cream in the other. You go to work day in and day out upset because your colleague got the promotion, instead of looking at your areas of growth and preparing for your 6 month review. You cannot afford to move forward being hindered by the emotions of your past. Depart from it! Reference to it… but do not dwell in it!

On the inside of this door, write things you are leaving in the past!

CHAPTER 7

Understanding the , (Commas) of life:

The times to pause, meditate, and prepare

Before God every takes you to the next level in life He will always give you a time of quite preparation. When we look at biblical stories one can notice how before a great work or change is done in someone's life; before transformation takes place, there is a moment of quietness and reflection with God. As you are coming to the close of this book I encourage you to learn the necessity of quiet and alone time with God. This entire book has brought us to this moment. Be able to develop and appreciate moments where you are able to do a self reflection. A comma represents the type of situation where you are forced to step back and reflect. This is a reflection not on external questions, dramas and seasons, but a reflection whose purpose is to give you internal peace. My ultimate goal is when you close the pages of this book the first time you will consistently be reminded to place a comma in some of your situations. I encourage you to revisit this book and the exercises you have completed and remind yourself to place commas in some situations.

Be encouraged that God has something great in store for you. The universe is waiting to open up the resources it has been allowed and shower you with them. Before you are able to get to the next level in yourself, your life and your quest towards destiny, you will be required to take some moments of reflection and self evaluation. I have adopted ancient Near Eastern and Middle Eastern practices of meditation. Many of you reading this book may be ready to stop reading and saying in your mind, "...isn't he a Baptist Pastor? We do not do that Buddhist, Toaist , monk stuff!" If you have not closed the book the bible says.....

[12]Let no man despise thy youth; but be thou an example of the believers, in word, in conversation, in charity, in spirit, in faith, in purity. [13]Till I come, give attendance to reading, to exhortation, to doctrine. [14]Neglect not the gift that is in thee, which was given thee by prophecy, with the laying on of the hands of the presbytery. **[15]Meditate upon these things; give thyself wholly to them; that thy profiting may appear to all.**

I Timothy 4:12-15

This scripture appears to have been my ministry theme since I started my ministry, at the age of fourteen, in 1999. Even Jesus took time away in silent prayer and meditation. If meditation is not your cup of tea, I am not encouraging you to do a Tina Turner and Num-YO-HO-Ren-Gey-Kio. But do take time to pause in quietness. The reason you cannot hear from God is because you are typically not listening. Many profess they pray and talk to God on a regular basis. Many prayer practices have become traditional and ritualistic. When was the last time you did not pray, but talked to God; without formality or fashion? I have been able to realize the commas in my life are moments of self reflection. When I am not concerned about protocols, obligations, or positions, I am able to approach life and God at another level.

At one point in life I was going through the motions and traditions of praying and seeking God. Then one day I realized my prayers began sounding the same. I realized I was not hearing God, and my life was not changing. It was not until I started studying the practices and lifestyles of those outside the Christian faith that I realized the power of the comma. The comma represents the pause in life that forces you to take a breath and make reflection. When I was in grade school I remember learning about the comma. I remember over exaggerating it when I would read. I was told the comma could be used to take a pause or breathe. I learned the comma was also used to continue a new dimension of the ideas presented or to introduce another idea. I remember consciously reading and anticipating to exercise the comma. This same anticipation carried over in my life practices. I make it a point to sit in quietness for a minimum of 10 minutes a day.

When you think about your day, how often do you listen to silence? You wake up to the TV being on. You hop in the car and the radio comes on. You go to your office or to your store and music's playing all day. You go out to dinner and not only is there music, but also a dozen other conversations in the background. You get back in your car and blast your favorite tunes for the evening. You get home to get on the phone with your friend to talk about gossip for the day. You turn on the television to catch up on the latest sitcom or reality television show. If it is not noise, you are constantly consumed with your thoughts while trying to figure out your life. You have thoughts about paying your bills. You have thoughts about fixing a relationship. If you are like me you find yourself talking to yourself while going throughout the day…. And I would have to write another chapter if I discussed how texting, ipods, myspace, facebook and cell phones prevent you from getting away to a quiet place! Sometimes you need to tell your life, "peace be still"!

When you step back and look

I am near sighted. I cannot see far away. There is one form of entertainment I love watching…magic. Growing up my mother used to love the magician David Copperfield. While she has seen a few of his shows, I have not been privileged to attend this great optical showcase. However, I have been to Las Vegas and seen a few smaller shows and skits. The amazing thing about entertainment magic is the skill needed to create an optical illusion. Everyone knows the acts performed are unreal. However, you are still amazed your eyes are seeing one thing, while your mind is affirming to you certain things are impossible. I hope not to offend anyone when I write this, but God is very similar to a magician. The father away you step from God's work, the more amazed you will be. God will begin to show you things that make no sense. But because He is God, they become your reality! When I speak about the commas of life, I speak about moments of regressing in order to view the situation from a different perspective.

I am at the position where I do not mind stepping back and allowing God to be God. You too should be able to understand and not be afraid to step back. I guarantee the moment you step back, you will find yourself like the child at the magic show; amazed, and perplexed because you do not understand how the act was done. How many situations has God brought you out of that left you scratching your head? My Elders would say, "I looked back and wondered how I got over?"

A best practice to develop is the art of taking one step back before you take two steps forward. Sometimes you must step back in order to reposition yourself. You do this in order to prevent rushing into something you are not prepared for. I will never forget the first time I went rock climbing. I was at a position on the wall where I was unable to move forward. There was nothing to grab above me. But there was something to grab diagonally across from me. However, I could not get to the other position on the wall until I went down a couple steps and repositioned myself. What is God challenging you to step back and away from before you move forward? I tell people all that time I experience an "out of body" experience. Call me crazy, but sometimes I will see myself, in present time, doing what I am doing at that moment. (It is ok to read that sentence again☺) I am not crazy, but I believe God has given me the ability to literally step back and analyze the choices I have before I make a decision. How much smoother, and how much less heart break could you avoid if you took a moment and stepped back?

If you had stepped back and looked at the person you were sleeping with, you would have seen they were no good. If you stepped away from your desk you would observed you are not at a place of happiness. If you were not consumed with the fact you can spend money; you could step back and see your spending habits are only taking you deeper into debt. One thing people have always complimented me on is my ability to observe. Before I enter any environment I will scope out as many, if not all, aspects of the scene. I do this because I want to know where I am and how I am to interact with my environment. The problem with many people is they enter into multiple environments diving head first without noting if they are in the shallow end. You have to stop allowing your impulses to be your guide; without allowing your spirit of discernment to guide you and be used.

I encourage you today to take a moment of reflection. Take a moment of true observation. A moment where you do not read into the situation, but we allow the situation to dialogue with you. Allow it to tell you what it is and its purpose in your life. Challenge yourself today to dialogue with your dilemma and chat with your conflict in order to understand what is really going on. I want to take this thought one step further to say, chat with the devil. You will be surprised when you step back and dialogue with the devil, what he is doing is not evil. You will uncover the fact that struggles have been put in place in order to work with the greater will of God. As I stated previously, when you step back and look at the situation you are able to view all the workings it takes in order to get the job done.

Understanding that the story continues

So often the greatest defeat you experience is the one you give yourself. How many situations can you admit it was not that you were defeated by life, but rather you gave up? Writing this chapter has been especially difficult for me. I had to do a self evaluation. I have wanted to give up countless times in my life. I have given up on many things in my life. As I walk through the streets. As I travel in the airports. As I walk and shop in the malls. As I even worship in multiple churches, there is a sense of hopelessness in the atmosphere. Beyond the smiles, marriages, jobs, houses, careers and worship experiences, there are many people, maybe some of you who have picked up this book, who wake up morning after morning with a sense of hopelessness. I dedicated this book to my grandmother. I felt hopeless when she passed in

October 1998. I felt a sense of hopelessness when my father was diagnosed with prostate cancer. I felt hopeless when I found myself sleeping on a bus stop in Atlanta. There are situations in our lives were giving up appears to be no other choice for us.

You made the assumption you were at the end of your story. You made the assumption it was time to throw in the towel. You have not walked into your calling or your destiny because you threw the towel in too early. I look back on situations in my life where it was not circumstance that hindered growth, but rather it was me. Either I was too lazy, too cautious, too afraid or just too stupid to realize I still had a long way to go. Place yourself in a mentality that speaks a clear path when there seems to be a dead end. I know there will be more opportunities to experience rock bottom. I also know in my ground zeros' is the potential to build a foundation. It is hard to see hope in some situations. It is hard to see peace when you are living in an abusive relationship. It is hard to see love when molestation and rape have left scars. It is hard to see prosperity when the bills outnumber the dollars on your paycheck. It is hard to see peace when there is hatred all around you. I must revisit the pervious chapter where I speak about perception in life. Using perception one could assume a sentence is coming to an end...but then you see the comma!

Maybe you are reading this book and finally realizing your story is not over. I want to encourage you before you throw in the towel and become defeated by yourself. There is more to your story and it is located after your comma. God will place a comma in your life so you can take a minute, reflect and then get back on track. You must learn how to uncover and acknowledge those commas in life. Commas are not signs it is over, but rather a new area of your life is ready to begin.

The power of Selah, Meditation and Reflection

We read the bible often and peruse over words we do not know and do not wish to understand. I remember in my youth reading the book of Psalms and always seeing the word "Selah". Being the child I was, I never thought to stop and look the word up. I thought it was some random phrase added at the end of the verse in order to give it an extra "Jesus/Spirit" to it. It was not until I got late into my ministry something told me to know what this word meant. When I found out it was a command, it wrecked my mind. Selah means… stop…. meditate… then act. The same scenario happens in your life. Many "selah" moments present themselves. Unfortunately they are consistently overlooked.

I am amazed at how loud life is. People seem as though they constantly need noise. Whether it be natural noise, television, radio, ipod, our just your own voice, you are constantly surrounded by noise. I encourage you to force yourself into meditation and reflection. I force myself to do it often. When I get overwhelmed, or there is too much on my agenda, or there are 1,000,007 things on my mind, I force myself to stop everything and regroup. Do not be afraid to put things off in order to reposition yourself. A hard lesson I learned over the years is that things can wait. I am neither the author nor finisher of anything. Many think if they are not doing it the show will cease. Rest assured if you close your eyes today, never to open them again, life will still go on. Many run to an early grave because they do not take time to selah. Many loose the law of gratitude because they do not take time to reflect on the blessings they have been given. I challenge you, if not once a day or once a week, once a month to sit in quietness. Tell your spouse to take the kids out for the evening. Turn the blackberry off. Keep the television and radio off. Ignore the doorbell. Light a candle and selah.

All this time I was supposed to be reading certain versus and meditating on them. The same thing happens in our lives and that is why God will place a comma or selah in our existence. I admonish all readers of the book to take a moment right now. Yes, you have my permission to put down this book. Where ever you are, for one minute, stop and clear your mind from everything. If you prefer to meditate and focus on something, focus on something you desire or wish to accomplish in your life. Rather than focusing on how you are going to get it done, focus on how you are going to let God work it out for you.

I often have selah/comma moments where, in spite of everything happening around me, I can always find a quite place. *"There is a quiet place; far from the rapid pace where God can soothe my troubled mind. Sheltered by tree and flower, there in my quiet hour, with Him, my cares are left behind. Whether a garden small, or on a mountain tall new strength and courage there I find there. Then from this quiet place I go prepared to face a new day, with love for all mankind"* (Quiet Place-Take6)

There is so much power in a selah moment. There is so much connectivity between you and the creator when you experience this pause in life. You will never hear the voice of God if you do not place yourself in the right environment to listen. I have received so much affirmation from God when I place myself in the moment of the comma. Sometimes my meditation is not focused on what to do in life, nor to get answers from God; it is in my comma moments God whispers His love, peace, joy, happiness, comfort, security and presence. The reason many feel as though God is not in their lives is because they never take the time to feel God's presence. They are so busy allowing their energy to be consumed by their environment; instead of allowing the energy of God to consume them. The Selah/comma moment can be intimidating. But it is necessary as you begin transition to the next moment in life…the life after the comma.

Proper preparation for transition

There is a reason I asked you to do the exercise in the previous chapter. Two things will help you in your transition to the next level of life. Preparation and location are key to progressing in life. Preparation should involve a plan from a moment of reflection. I challenge you, as you come to the final pages of this book, to prepare yourself for the great things that are to come in your life. Growing up my mother would hound on the scripture of writing the vision and making it plain. Before you complete the final exercise in this book I challenge you not to write for the sake of writing or because you feel commanded to. I want you to take a moment to hear from God. Listen for words regarding your calling, passion, purpose and destiny in life. Before you create any blueprints for your life refer to the great architect and master builder. In your moment of preparation observe things that are not working. Understand the reason things are not working is because God does not want them to. Progress cannot happen without proper preparation. Decisions should not be made, nor a plan formed without having a clear mind. People rush into things without considering the path to take. With any transition in life there must be a moment of preparation.

You must make sure you are in the right position when transition is ready to take place in your life. You will miss the perfect wave because you are not in the right location to catch the right current. What makes a comma different from any other punctuation is it is not placed at the end of a sentence. Rather the comma is strategically placed somewhere along the middle of the sentence. Regardless of where you are in life, now is a good place to place a comma. That fact you have picked up this white book and have made it to the final pages, I thank you. But most importantly I thank you for accepting the challenge to relearn the grammar lesson on life. Wherever you are in your relationships, education, career or spiritual walk, now is a good time to place a comma. Now is a good location to transform your life into a life that is meaningful and purposeful. Now is a great time to take your before and create an after. Now is the moment where you refuse to accept closure, but rather formulate a new beginning. Know when God places a comma in your life you are half way through the lesson. All you must do with your life now is get past the comma! The comma is used in grammar to transition from one thought to another, while in real life it is used to transition you from one level to the next.

After a serious moment of reflection and meditation write to the left of the eye the new outlook, perspective and vision for your life. Begin your vision statements with "I can see myself..."

CHAPTER 8

Life After the Comma!

More to your story will be revealed! Notice when you drive at night how the lights on your car allow you to see approximately 200ft ahead. Amazingly 200ft is all you need to drive from New York to Los Angeles and back. You do not need a laser beam to illuminate the entire path to your destination. All you need is a little light and a lot of faith. I encourage you to desire knowing the big picture, but first seek the purpose of the paint brush and the easel in your life. I hope you did not pick up this book expecting to find the answers to living a magical life. I do hope you were able to receive from this book a new perspective on how to approach your life.

There was a point in life where I wanted God to show me everything upfront. I wanted to know everything about everything going on in my life. Then there was a day I realized the greatest portion of the adventure was the matter of discovery. There are great and greater things coming in your life, but you have to discover them. There is a reason scripture talks about seeing through a glass darkly and then face to face.

Make the affirmation daily that the rest will come. Your prayers are not going unanswered, but rather what you are asking may still need to be discovered. Get to the point in your life where you quit asking God for answers. Rather begin to ask for revelation. Instead of asking God to remove you from drama, make it your prayer to ask for endurance. Instead of requesting closure, allow God to show you the potential that lies in every situation.

God has more for you but you cannot assume the story is over while it is still going on. Do not accept defeat when you still have many rounds to fight. I find it amazing how people not only give up, but they give up right in the middle of the battle. Understand a battle is exactly that. The war, however, still needs to be won. I guarantee if you put the energy forth, you will discover there is more for your tomorrow if you can just get through today. Get ready to receive the fruit of your seed and the reward from your labor.

Assumptions kill a lot of your dreams. Recall the last time you assumed something. Now see if that assumption was in your favor or out of your favor. More than likely it was out of favor for you. In my many years of management, sales and ministry, I have learned the importance of making assumptions in my favor. If you are going to make an assumption, assume the situation to your advantage. Do not make an assumption that because one school did not work you are doomed never to get a degree…maybe you need to change your major. Do not make the assumption that because your last relationship did not work there is something wrong with you…maybe your love is what was unappreciated. Do not assume you will never have relationship with God because of an addiction or emotional hang up…maybe God wants to use your mess as the foundation for your ministry. Do not assume where you are now is the end result. Affirm to yourself daily, as I do, that every day brings forth new possibility and greater potential. The only thing that is ever over in your life is yesterday. Determine to get to the end; which is after the comma.

In order to make it through some aspects of your life understand the importance of not focusing on what appears to be right now. Get to a position where you view the greater good in all things. Regardless of what the situation looks like there is God and good somewhere in it. When you change your focus, you can change your perception. When you change your perception, you can change your attitude. When you change your attitude, you can change your actions. When you change your actions, you can change your results. When your results change, you will begin to live a life of abundance, prosperity, true joy, love and fulfillment. But you first have to stop accepting things for their face value. If life is handing you nothing but lumps of coal, pile them up, put them in the fire and add some pressure to them. There is potential for a diamond. If you receive nothing else from these final pages, walk away enlightened. As long as you replay the movie of your memories, the delivery of your destiny will never become reality. Make it your decision to consider choices that give you longevity with success. The awesome thing about this book is that it has helped, and will help, thousands of individuals; by giving them hope for a brighter and greater future not dictated by their past.

You can get caught up in final punctuations. You can think the story is over because you see ending instead of transition. As I close this book I want you to view life, not from the position of an ended sentence. Rather, I want you to view the sentence as over; but much still needs to be read in your story. I encourage you to adopt the attitude that every day will bring about a new opportunity for great potential to manifest success, happiness, joy, love and prosperity. You may have picked up this book with a great sense of hopelessness in your life. You may have told yourself on multiple occasions, "what is, is" and "what will be, will be". I encourage you to say, "what is, is" and "what will be, will only come through experiencing the adventure". Revisit the pages of this book often and share the message with others. Do not hold on to this new idea of living and perception as some great secret. Desire all around you would experience what you will begin to experience because of the concepts discussed in *"After the Comma: A Grammar Lesson on Life"*.

The main idea of this book is simple. Develop a "comma mentality"- Things are better on the other side!

I Love You and God Loves You!

W. T. Dandridge

A Special Thanks to…

God who continues to give me strength, wisdom and courage to continue on my destiny quest.

Wallace and Kathleen Dandridge for your support and love throughout my entire life and ministry. I love you MOM and DAD!

To my siblings Michael, Rose-Eva, and Amanda thank you for encouraging me and encouraging my example.

Rev. Dr. Ralph D. White for licensing me to the ministry.

Dr. Philip Dunston for trusting me & helping me to develop my love for the psychology of religion. We have more books to write!

Pastor Michael Palmer (Lisa and lil Mike) and the New Friendship Family…Home is always the best supporter!

Dr. William E. Flippin and the Greater Piney Grove Family your example of excellence is a model to my ministry.

Pastor Robert L. Hodo and the New Morning Light Family for being good soil to plant good seed (Shout out to 7th Dynasty)!

To YOU for reading this work and supporting my ministry!

Rosie Brown…The Love of My Life R.I.P (10/98)

Made in the USA
Charleston, SC
22 October 2011